DEAR PETER

Miniature Letters by Beatrix Potter

FREDERICK WARNE

FREDERICK WARNE

Published by the Penguin Group
Penguin Books Ltd., 80 Strand, London WC2R 0RL, England
Penguin Group (USA) Inc., 375 Hudson Street, New York, New York 10014, USA
Penguin Books Australia Ltd., 250 Camberwell Road, Camberwell, Victoria 3124, Australia
Penguin Books Canada Ltd., 90 Eglinton Avenue East, Suite 700, Toronto, Ontario, Canada M4P 2Y3
Penguin Books India (P) Ltd., 11 Community Centre, Panchsheel Park, New Delhi 110017
Penguin Books (NZ) Ltd., 67 Apollo Drive, Rosedale, North Shore 0632, New Zealand
Penguin Books (South Africa) (Pty) Ltd., 24 Sturdee Avenue Rosebank 2196, South Africa

Penguin Books Ltd., Registered Offices: 80 Strand, London WC2R 0RL, England

Website: www.peterrabbit.com

Copyright © Frederick Warne & Co., 2012
Some material previously published in *Yours Affectionately, Peter Rabbit*,
published by Frederick Warne in 1983

001 - 10 9 8 7 6 5 4 3 2 1

Manufactured in China

ISBN 978-0-7232-6767-6

Contents

INTRODUCTION

If you've picked up this book, you are probably a fan of Beatrix Potter. So, like us, you will know that Beatrix was an exceptionally talented writer and illustrator who created twenty-three tales of delightful naughtiness. So enjoyable are her stories that when you reach the final page, you are left wanting more. You have no doubt asked yourself, 'So, what happened next? Did Peter Rabbit stay away from Mr. McGregor's garden? Did Squirrel Nutkin grow back his tail?'. And you might have guessed that things did *not* go that smoothly, and the proof is contained within the pages of this book.

ABOVE: *Lucie Carr and her sister Kathleen.*

Over the course of a few years, between 1907 and 1912, Beatrix wrote an invented correspondence featuring her famous characters, telling of their continuing adventures and mishievous deeds. The letters were shaped so that they could be folded up into tiny envelopes with drawn-on stamps and sent out to real children, sometimes in a doll-size mailbag or a bright red enameled miniature post box. The letters were sent to many different children, some of whom were family friends of Beatrix, and some simply readers who had written to their favourite author. One little girl, Lucie Carr, is the same Lucie who appears in *The Tale of Mrs. Tiggy-Winkle*.

'Some of the letters were very funny,' Beatrix herself said. We agree and think you will too!

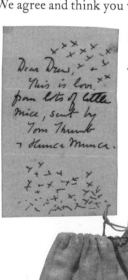

LEFT: *Miniature letter from Tom Thumb and Hunca Munca to Drew Fayle, Kylemore, Dublin.*

LEFT AND ABOVE: *A miniature mail bag and tin post box made by Beatrix Potter for use with her miniature letters to children.*

9

WHO'S WHO IN THE LETTERS

All of the characters who appear in these letters feature in Beatrix Potter's famous tales. To get the most out of this book, we recommend that you read the original tales.

who appears in
The Tale of Peter Rabbit

who appears in
The Tale of Squirrel Nutkin

who appears in
The Tale of Squirrel Nutkin

who appears in
The Tale of Two Bad Mice

who appears in
The Tale of Two Bad Mice

who appears in
The Tale of Mrs. Tiggy-Winkle

who appears in
The Tale of Mr. Jeremy Fisher

who appears in
The Tale of Samuel Whiskers

who appear in
The Tale of The Flopsy Bunnies

The Peter Rabbit Picture Letter

The most important letter written by Beatrix Potter was the one that started her on her path to creating some of the best-loved children's books of all time. The original Peter Rabbit picture letter was written by Beatrix in 1893 to cheer up a poorly boy called Noel Moore. We present it here in its entirety for your enjoyment!

Eastwood Dunkeld
Sep 4th 93

My dear Noel,
            I don't know what to
write to you, so I shall tell you a story
            about four little rabbits.
                        whose names were—

Flopsy, Mopsy Cottontail

and Peter

They lived with their mother in a
sand bank under the root of a
big fir tree.

13

"Now, my dears", said old Mrs Bunny 'you may go into the field or down the lane, but don't go into Mr McGregor's garden.'

Flopsy, Mopsy & Cottontail, who were good little rabbits went down the lane to gather blackberries, but Peter, who was very naughty

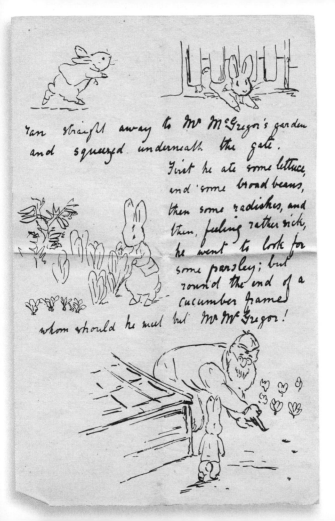

ran straight away to Mr McGregor's garden and squeezed underneath the gate.

First he ate some lettuce, and some broad beans, then some radishes, and then, feeling rather sick, he went to look for some parsley; but round the end of a cucumber frame whom should he meet but Mr McGregor!

15

Mr McGregor was planting out young cabbages but he jumped up & ran after Peter waving a rake & calling out 'Stop thief!'

Peter was most dreadfully frightened & rushed all over the garden, for he had forgotten the way back to the gate.
He lost one of his shoes among the cabbages

and the other shoe amongst the potatoes.
After losing them he ran on four legs &
went faster, so that I think he would

have got away altogether; if he had not
unfortunately run into a gooseberry net
and got caught fast by the large buttons
on his jacket. It was a blue jacket with
brass buttons; quite new.

Mr. McGregor came up with a basket which
he intended to pop on the top of Peter,
but Peter wriggled out just in time,
       leaving his jacket behind,

and this time he found the gate,
slipped underneath and ran home
safely.

Mr. Mc.Gregor hung up the little jacket & shoes for a scarecrow, to frighten the black birds.

Peter was ill during the evening, in consequence of over eating himself. His mother put him to bed and gave him a dose of camomile tea,

but Hopsy, Mopsy, and Cottontail
had bread and milk and blackberries
for supper.   I am coming
back to London next Thursday, so
I hope I shall see you soon, and
the new baby. I remain, dear Noel,
yours affectionately

Beatrix Potter.

PETER RABBIT'S CORRESPONDENCE

After his fur-raising adventures in *The Tale of Peter Rabbit*, did Peter learn his lesson and stay away from the McGregors' vegetables? We fear not...

Mr. McGregor,
Gardener's Cottage.

Dear Sir,
I write to ask whether your
spring cabbages are ready?
Kindly reply by return and
oblige.

Yrs. truly,
Peter Rabbit.

Master P. Rabbit,
Under Fir Tree.

Sir,
I rite by desir of my Husband
Mr. McGregor who is in Bedd
with a Cauld to say if you
Comes heer agane we will
inform the Polisse.

Jane McGregor.

P.S. I have bort a new py-Dish,
itt is vary Large.

Master Benjamin Bunny,
The Warren.

Dear Cousin Benjamin,

I have had a very ill written
letter from Mrs. McGregor she
says Mr. M. is in bed with a cold
will you meet me at the corner
of the wood near their garden
at 6 this evening?
In haste.

Yr. aff. cousin,
Peter Rabbit.

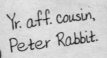

One lucky reader was fortunate enough to receive a letter from Peter Rabbit himself!

Master Drew,
Kylimore.

Dear Master Drew,
I am pleased to hear you like Miss Potter's books. Miss Potter is drawing pigs & mice. She says she has drawn enough rabbits. But I am to be put into one picture at the end of the pig book.

Yr. aff friend,
xx Peter

xxxxx xxxx

Squirrel Nutkin's Correspondence

Poor Squirrel Nutkin repents of his rudeness to Old Brown after the owl broke off his tail. But will politeness be enough to get it back again?

Nutkin pulled so very hard that his tail broke in two...

Mr. Brown,
Owl Island.

Sir,
I should esteem it a favour if
you would let me have back my
tail, as I miss it very much.
I would pay postage.

Yrs. truly,
Squirrel Nutkin.

29

Mr. Old Brown Esq,
Owl Island.

Dear Sir,

I should be extremely obliged if you could kindly send back a tail which you have had for some time. It is fluffy brown with a white tip. I wrote to you before about it, but perhaps I did not address the letter properly. I will pay the postage.

Yrs. respectfully,
Sq. Nutkin.

Old Mr. Brown Esq;,
Owl Island.

Dear Sir,
I should be exceedingly obliged if you will let me have back my tail, I will gladly pay 3 bags of nuts for it if you will please post it back to me, I have written to you twice Mr. Brown, I think I did not give my address, it is Derwent Bay Wood.

Yrs. respectfully,
Sq. Nutkin.

31

The Right Honourable
Old Brown Esq.,
Owl Island.

Sir,

I write respectfully to beg that you
will sell me back my tail, I am so
uncomfortable without it, and I have
heard of a tailor who would sew it on
again. I would pay three bags of
nuts for it. Please Sir, Mr. Brown, send
it back by post & oblige.

Yrs. respectfully,
Sq. Nutkin.

O. Brown Esq., M.P.

Owl Island.

Dear Sir,

I write on behalf of my brother Nutkin
to beg that as a great favour you
would send him back his tail. He never
makes - or asks - riddles now, and he
is truly sorry that he was so rude. Trusting
that you continue to enjoy good health,
I remain,

Yr. obedient servant,
Twinkleberry Squirrel.

Master Squirrel Nutkin,
Derwent Bay Wood.

Mr. Brown writes to say that he cannot reply to letters as he is asleep. Mr. Brown cannot return the tail. He ate it some time ago; it nearly choked him. Mr. Brown requests Nutkin not to write again, as his repeated letters are a nuisance.

LUCINDA DOLL'S CORRESPONDENCE

Poor Lucinda Doll! After Tom Thumb and Hunca Munca wreaked havoc in her beautiful house in *The Tale of Two Bad Mice*, they have decided to make amends by being helpful instead. How long can this happy arrangement last?

Mrs. Thomas Thumb,
Mouse Hole.

Miss Lucinda Doll will require
Hunca Munca to come for the whole
day on Saturday. Jane Dollcook has
had an accident. She has broken the
soup tureen and both her wooden legs.

Miss Lucinda Doll,
Doll's House

Honoured Madam,
Would you forgive my asking whether you
can spare a feather bed? The feathers are
all coming out of the one we stole from
your house. If you can spare another, me
& my wife would be truly grateful.

Yr. obedient humble servant,
Thomas Thumb

P.S. Me & my wife are grateful to you
for employing her as char-woman I hope
that she continues to give satisfaction.

P.P.S. Me & my wife would be grateful
for any old clothes, we have 9 of a
family at present.

Then those mice set to work to do all the mischief they could...

Mr T. Thumb,
Mouse Hole

Miss Lucinda Doll has received Tom Thumb's appeal, but she regrets to inform Tom Thumb that she has never had another feather bed for herself. She also regrets to say that Hunca Munca forgot to dust the mantelpiece on Wednesday.

Miss Lucinda Doll,
Doll's House.

Honoured Madam,
I am sorry to hear that my wife
forgot to dust the mantelpiece, I have
whipped her. Me & my wife would be
very grateful for another kettle, the
last one is full of holes. Me & my
wife do not think that it was made
of tin at all. We have nine of a family
at present & they require hot water.
    I remain honoured madam,

Yr. obedient servant,
        Thomas Thumb

Mrs. Tom Thumb,
Mouse Hole.

Miss Lucinda Doll will be obliged if
Hunca Munca will come half an hour
earlier than usual on Tuesday morning,
as Tom Kitten is expected to sweep the
kitchen chimney at 6 o'clock. Lucinda
wishes Hunca Munca to come not later
than 5.45 a.m.

Miss Lucinda Doll,
Doll's House

Honoured Madam,
I have received your note for which
I thank you kindly, informing me that
T. Kitten will arrive to sweep the
chimney at 6. I will come punctually
at 7. Thanking you for past favours I
am, honoured Madam, your obedient
humble Servant,

Hunca Munca

42

However, just when we thought that Hunca Munca and Tom Thumb had redeemed themselves, we realise that all is *not* what it seems...

GINGER & PICKLES LTD.

Messrs Ginger & Pickles—Grocers—in account with Miss Lucinda Doll, Doll's House

4 thimblefuls of brown sugar	@ 2d	=	1 farthing
6 thimblefuls of white sugar	@ 2d	=	1½ farthings
3 tastes stilton Cheese	@ ⅓ per lb.		say ¹⁄₁₀ farthing

2 ⁶⁄₁₀ farthings—
2½d (about)

with Messrs G & P^s comp^{ts} & thanks.

Ginger and Pickles retired to the back parlour. They did accounts.

Miss Lucinda Doll has received Messrs Pickle & Ginger's account, about which there is some mistake. She has lived for some months upon German plaster provisions & saw dust, and had given no order for the groceries mentioned in the bill.

Miss Lucinda Doll,
Doll's House.

GINGER & PICKLES LTD.

Messrs Ginger & Pickles beg to apologize
to Miss Lucinda Doll for their mistake.
The goods were selected (& taken away
from the shop) to the order of Miss Doll.
But Messrs Ginger & Pickles' young man
had his doubts at the time. The messenger
will not be served again.

MRS. TIGGY-WINKLE'S CORRESPONDENCE

When you're a busy hedgehog, it can be hard to keep everything straight, and Mrs. Tiggy-winkle needs her customers to be understanding.

Mrs Tiggy Winkle,
Cat Bells.

Dear Madam,
Though unwilling to hurt the feelings of
another widow, I really cannot any
longer put up with starch in my pocket
handkerchiefs. I am sending this one
back to you, to be washed again. Unless
the washing improves next week I shall
(reluctantly) feel obliged to change
my laundry.

Yrs. truly,
Josephine Rabbit.

Mrs. Rabbit,
Sand Bank,
Under Fir-Tree

If you please'm,
Indeed I apologise sincerely for the
starchiness & hope you will forgive me if
you please mum, indeed it is Tom Titmouse
and the rest of them; they do want their
collar that starchy if you please mum my
mind do get mixed up. If you please I
will wash the clothes without charge for a
fortnight if you will give another trial to
your obedient servant & washerwoman,

Tiggy Winkle.

Mrs. Tiggy Winkle,
Cat Bells.

Dear Mrs. Tiggy Winkle,
I am much pleased with the getting up of the children's muslin frocks. Your explanation about the starch is perfectly satisfactory & I have no intention of changing my laundry at present. Nobody washes flannels like Mrs. Tiggy Winkle.

With kind regards,
yrs. truly,
Josephine Rabbit.

Poor Mrs. Tiggy-winkle is in such a fluster that she even writes to young reader Drew Fayle to see if *he* has received the correct washing...

Master D. Fayle,

Kylimore,

Co. Dublin.

Dear Drew,

I have got that mixed up with this week's wash! Have you got Mrs. Flopsy Bunny's shirt or Mr. Jeremy Fisher's apron? Instead of your pocket handkerchief—I mean to say Mrs. Flopsy Bunny's apron. Everything is got all mixed up in wrong bundles. I will buy more safety pins.

Yr. aff. Washerwoman

T. Winkle

Master D. Fayle,
Kylimore

Dear Drew,
I hope that your washing is done to please
you? I consider that Mrs. Tiggy Winkle is
particularly good at ironing collars; but she
does mix things up at the wash. I have got
a shirt marked J. F. instead of an apron.
Have you lost a shirt at the wash? It is 3
inches long. My apron is much larger and
marked F. B.

Yrs.
Flopsy Bunny.

Mrs. Tiggy Winkle,
Cat Bells.

Mr. J. Fisher regrets that he has to complain about the washing. Mrs. T. W. has sent home an immense white apron with tapes instead of Mr. J. F's best new shirt. The apron is marked F. B.

Jan. 22. 1910.

Mrs. Tiggy Winkle,

Cat Bells.

Mr. J. Fisher regrets to have to complain
again about the washing. Mrs. T. Winkle has
sent home an enormous handkerchief
marked 'D. Fayle' instead of the tablecloth
marked J. F.

If this continues every week, Mr. J. Fisher
will have to get married, so as to have the
washing done at home.

Correspondence Concerning Mr. Jeremy Fisher

It seems that Drew Fayle was interested in the welfare of *all* Beatrix Potter's characters. He wrote to her saying that Mr. Jeremy Fisher needs a wife. But who would want that job?

Master D. Fayle,
Kylimore.

Dear Master Drew,

I hear that you think that there ought to
be a 'Mrs. J. Fisher'. Our friend is at
present taking mud baths at the bottom of
the pond, which may be the reason why
your letter has not been answered quick by
return. I will do my best to advise him,
but I fear he remembers the sad fate of his
elder brother who disobeyed his mother,

and he was gobbled up by a lily white
duck! If my friend Jeremy Fisher gets
married, I will certainly tell you, & send
a bit of wedding cake. One of our friends is
going into the next book. He is fatter than
Jeremy; and he has shorter legs.

Yrs. with compliments,
Sir Isacc Newton.

Master Drew Fayle,
Kylimore.

Dear Master Drew,
I hear that you are interested in the domestic arrangements of our friend Jeremy Fisher. I am of the opinion that his dinner parties would be much more agreeable if there were a lady to preside at the table. I do not care for roast grasshoppers. His housekeeping and cookery do not come up to the standard to which I am accustomed at the Mansion House.

Yrs. truly,
Alderman Pt. Tortoise.

Master D. Fayle,
Kylimore,
Co. Dublin.

Dear Master Drew,
In answer to your very kind inquiry, I live alone; I am not married. When I bought my sprigged waistcoat & my maroon tail-coat, I had hopes ... But I am alone ... If there were a 'Mrs. Jeremy Fisher' she might object to snails. It is some satisfaction to be able to have as much water & mud in the house as a person likes.

Thanking you for your touching inquiry,

Yr. devoted friend,
Jeremiah Fisher.

Master Drew Fayle,
Kylimore, Co. Dublin.

Dear Master Drew,
If you please Sir I am a widow; and I think it is very wrong that there is not any Mrs. Jeremy Fisher, but I would not marry Mr. Jeremy not for worlds, the way he does live in that house all slippy-sloppy; not any lady would stand it, and not a bit of good starching his cravats.

Yr. obedient washerwoman,
Tiggy Winkle.

Mr. Samuel Whiskers' Correspondence

Farmer Potatoes wants the rats out of his barn! But where can Samuel Whiskers and his enormous family go?

To Samuel Rat,
High Barn.

Sir,
I hereby give you one day's
notice to quit my barn & stables
and byre, with your wife, children,
grand children & great grand
children to the latest generation.

signed: William Potatoes, Farmer.

witness: Gilbert Cat & John
            Stoat-Ferret.

As for Farmer Potatoes, he has been driven nearly distracted.

Farmer Potatoes,
The Priddings.

Sir,
I have opened a letter
addressed to one Samuel Rat.
If Samuel Rat means me, I inform
you I shall not go, and you can't
turn us out.

Yrs. etc.
Samuel Whiskers.

Mr. Obediah Rat,
Barley Mill.

Dear Friend Obediah,
Expect us – bag and baggage – at
9 o'clock in the morning. Am sorry
to come upon you suddenly; but my
Landlord William Potatoes has
given me one day's notice to quit. I
am of opinion that it is not legal
& I could sit till Candlemas
because the notice is not
addressed to my proper sur-name.
I would stand up to William
Potatoes, but my wife will not face
John Stoat-Ferret, so we have
decided on a midnight flitting
as it is full-moon. I think there

are 96 of us, but am not certain.
Had it been the Mayday term we
could have gone to the Field
Drains, but it is out of the question
at this season. Trusting that the
meal bags are full.

Yr. obliged friend,
Samuel Whiskers.

68

THE FLOPSY BUNNIES' CORRESPONDENCE

Sometimes Beatrix Potter got too busy to answer her own letters. Here, the kind Flopsy Bunnies decide to help her out.

Miss M. Moller,
Caldecote Grange,
Biggleswade.

My dear Miss Moller,
I am pleased to hear that you like the
F. Bunnies, because some people do think
there has been too much bunnies; and
there is going to be some more!
My family will appear again in the next book;
and Cottontail is put in because you asked
after her, which me and Cottontail thanks you
for kind inquiries and remembrance.

Yrs. respectful
Flopsy Bunny.

Dear Madam

My wife Mrs. Flopsy Bunny has replied to your inquiries, because Miss potter will attend to nothing but hatching spring chickens; there is another hatch chirping this evening. And she is supposed to be doing a Book, about us and the Fox; but she does not get on; neither has she answered all her Xmas letters yet.

Yrs
B. Bunny.

Master John Hough,
88 Darenth Road,
N.W.

Dear Master John Hough,

I and my Family (6) are writing to you because Miss Potter has got no stamps left and she has got a cold, we think Miss Potter is lazy. I think you are a fine big boy; my children are small rabbits at present.

Yrs. respectfully,
Mrs. Flopsy Bunny.

They had a large family, and they were very
improvident and cheerful.

Dear Master
John Hough,

I wish you a Merry
Christmas! I am going to
have an apple for my
Christmas dinner & some
celery tops. The cabbages
are all frosted but there
is lots of hay.

Yrs. aff.
First Flopsy Bunny.
XXXXXXX

Dear Master John,
I wish you the same as my eldest brother, and I am going to have the same dinner.

yrs. aff.
2nd. FLOPSY BUNNY.

xxxxxx

Dear Master Hough,

I wish you the compliments of the season. We have got new fur tippets for Christmas.

yrs. aff.
3rd. (Miss) F. Bunny.
XXX

Dear master
John,
I have not
learned to rite
propperly.

Love from
4th Miss F. Bunny

XXXXX
5th Miss F. Bunny

XXX

with his love,
from the 6th Master F. B.

Affectionately yours

x